Expressions From Within

by Larry B. Stell

SCRIPTOR HOUSE
THE EPITOME OF GREATNESS

Scriptor House LLC

2810 N Church St Wilmington, Delaware, 19802

www.scriptorhouse.com

Phone: +1302-205-2043

Published by Scriptor House LLC

Paperback ISBN: 979-8-88692-220-2

eBook ISBN: 979-8-88692-221-9

Expressions From Within

by Larry B. Stell

CONTENTS

Dedicated to Liane Claudia Stell, my daughter. She resides in Bad Kreuznach, Germany where she and her husband own a trucking business. She is a trained physical therapist but now owns her fingernail manicuring shop at their home,

Bad Kreuznach, Germany. Liane is a German citizen.

foreword

I composed these poems spontaneously. If I am inspired,
I pounce upon that seed, theme, or idea then write each
poem in a short period of time. My inspiration comes
from a broad background of travel, intermingling with
other cultures and languages, and a reverent respect for my
fellow man and nature!

I WALKED WHERE HEMINGWAY AND FAULKNER WALKED

I walked where Hemingway wrote his book

"Across the River and Into the Woods"

It was a great adventure also that led me abroad

It is rapture to have lived so near where the river lay flat

And the colonel shot the ducks from a barrel that day!

Compare Hemingway with Faulkner

Two great minds illuminating literature

Literature exquisite and bright!

Hemingway so adept and clear

Faulkner so complex within Compare the two,

But I walked where Hemingway walked and wrote

In Italy, the north, "Across the River and Into the Woods!"

The setting shone so bright!

William Faulkner and a book like "Pylon," stirs the soul

That book, lucid, yet complex, with depiction of a city so warm

Intriguing New Orleans, a city with European taste

I also lived there and saw the setting of that 30s book!

Compare the two bright stars, if I really dare?

Hemingway, so simplistic in style,

Faulkner so complex, so deep within!

Have the two ever been so adroitly compared?

I think not; it is an avenue to be discovered, to vastly explore

Why does one make the comparison?

Because great minds have achieved and excelled

These two intensely rewarded,

already have received their accolades,

Already acknowledged

I walked there, in Italy and all its past

But do we dare question the mind within, of William Faulkner?

Eternally to be explored and dissected in depth

Only the South can tell, his vastness may someday

Produce that one again who can achieve his mode

And again, Hemingway, widely traveled, visions broad and wide

But only Hemingway and Faulkner are models so great

Often explored and exciting to compare!

A CHILD SO DEAR

A mistake of mine
To hold back my love
Then realize a song to pine;
Overfilled with life's great sign
A gracious view, from way above.

My feeble attempt to hold so dear;
Lost sometimes in frequent dreams,
I long for contact and wish to be near;
Now I long that she were here,
She could share in a life that streams.

Speak as often as you can
And chide or evaluate;
A life seeking a viable plan
So often dreaming when I can,
I see her now, grown and great!

A WORLD OF BEAUTY

Our world outside shines brightly

So that everyday is like a rainbow

Clouds shine underneath the sun lightly

The earth about us in a lovely glow

A world captivated by nature's beauty

Like a ship sailing briskly out to sea

A crew sets a course with love and duty

This world alone belongs to you and me!

A WORLD UNEPLORED

Wanderlust! It is a seed within

Through it evolves challenges

Challenges yet unseen

Whether it is in a society unknown or in a village afar,

The knowledge to be gained lies ahead

And the discoveries to be found enhance the soul

The value of exploration lies within us all

The haste to find the beauty of a world unexplored

Whether in youth or maturity lies within the soul

The resonance of that world leads on

Many have satisfied the curiosity; but most are not there

Exploration of a myriad of places and things afar

Propel us to a place that satisfies curiosity of life

And through this desire we are lead

To a world vastly unexplored!

ANNA

She was a part of my life, more than two years ago
Her almond shaped eyes still shine in the sunlight
Her soul is unique because it is strong and
Often resists the most acute aspects of fate
Her soul is authentic and thrives on sincerity
Anna, so world aware, spent a part of her life
In Africa so rare, with Tanzania, a part of her youth
Where she learned of cultures in strife
Her life in Africa exposed her to cultures unique
But a return to her home in our nation so great
Proved to her with God determining her fate,
That a provincial setting is not her love, because
The world out there must determine her taste
While she explores what waits, in Europe, and
Other continents so rare, plus many a culture
To test her desires for travel and quest
For a life with someone who will challenge
This Anna and accentuate her best!

CHALLENGES OF LIFE

As time goes on the tasks eternally grow
Life moves forward, the challenges complex
Then like melting snow, memories descend
And their sweetness ascend in the mind
While challenges mount with change,
But are met with age so wise, while before
Our youthful minds saw them as fleeting moments
Of inane conflicts, slowing down our progress
But now challenges become the trials of life,
Asserting their restrictions and impugning
Our momentum that once prevailed
And elevated our lives toward momentous goals
Eternally imbued by nature's cloak, veiled
By the challenges ubiquitous, but always there!

CHARMS

Your charms are endearing

A halo of light enhances your soul

The splendor of life enriches your charms

Enjoy the motivation imbued in your psychic

Because it will enhance the wisdom of your being!

COMPATIBILITY

Compatibility evolves from love and self-awareness
Love and respect emit the ray of consciousness
A ray of consciousness about to be released
Time is accountable to the exposure and involvement
Intertwined with a never ending exchange
An exchange of ideas, reciprocating dialogues, and respect!
Trust and mutual determination often exhibit the cement
That makes us more tolerable, more fluid, and more aware!
Assumption of trust, belief, and accessibility of ideal contact
Relieves the conflict of distrust and disposed hate
While we lust in the desire of ideal achievement,
We can only seek the road to true compatibility,
Never ending, because of the constant rush of externalism
All we do must evolve to a state of true compatibility
Because with it the threads of veiled individuality
pounce upon us!

CONFLICT

The opposition is intellectual,
But the contrast is not so great
Our lives are rich and interwoven with a halo of richness,
Steeped in the roots of European culture and beauty,
Adopted through intense exposure!
The readjustment of life back home,
Enriched by languages and culture from afar,
Entice us both to drop the veil of provincial dependency
But the ebullition lurks in your soul!
Sometimes in my own, although faintly!
To readjust to a culture once embedded in our souls,
Is a challenge that confronts us both with an intense rapture!
The structure of our roors is embellished by Europe's tinge!
We have both embellished our lives with languages anew
But now we must strive to transcend and improve with a grace
And quality, most needed, like a breed of embryonic excellence,
Imbued with genes from opposing strands!
We must take heed, after the enlightenment of confluence
from afar,
And can only strive to expand our riches, and share them
with grace and dignity,
Extrapolated from God's own universe, enamored by our
enhanced souls!

CONSOLATION

I console your feelings
As they intertwine in mine
Your composure intends to
Blend your mood within
But the path to solace
Is more than just restrain
Or mirth to veil your pain
The path to consolation
Comes from within and without
And emits a love of self
As it opens your heart
To the beauty of life all about!

CONTEMPORARY IDEAS

Contemporary ideas have plagued me

From childhood to adulthood

They range from the small to the large

From the micro to the macro

Contemporary ideas indulge our existence

Whether from within or without

Contemporary ideas will take us through

The pitfalls of life and death

Whether in ecstasy or in love

Our plans will evolve

With ideas elevated aloft

And desires so great

Contemporary ideas will also invade us

Sometimes from within and sometimes from without

They enhance our existence, withstanding our time

Contemporary ideas will release our stress

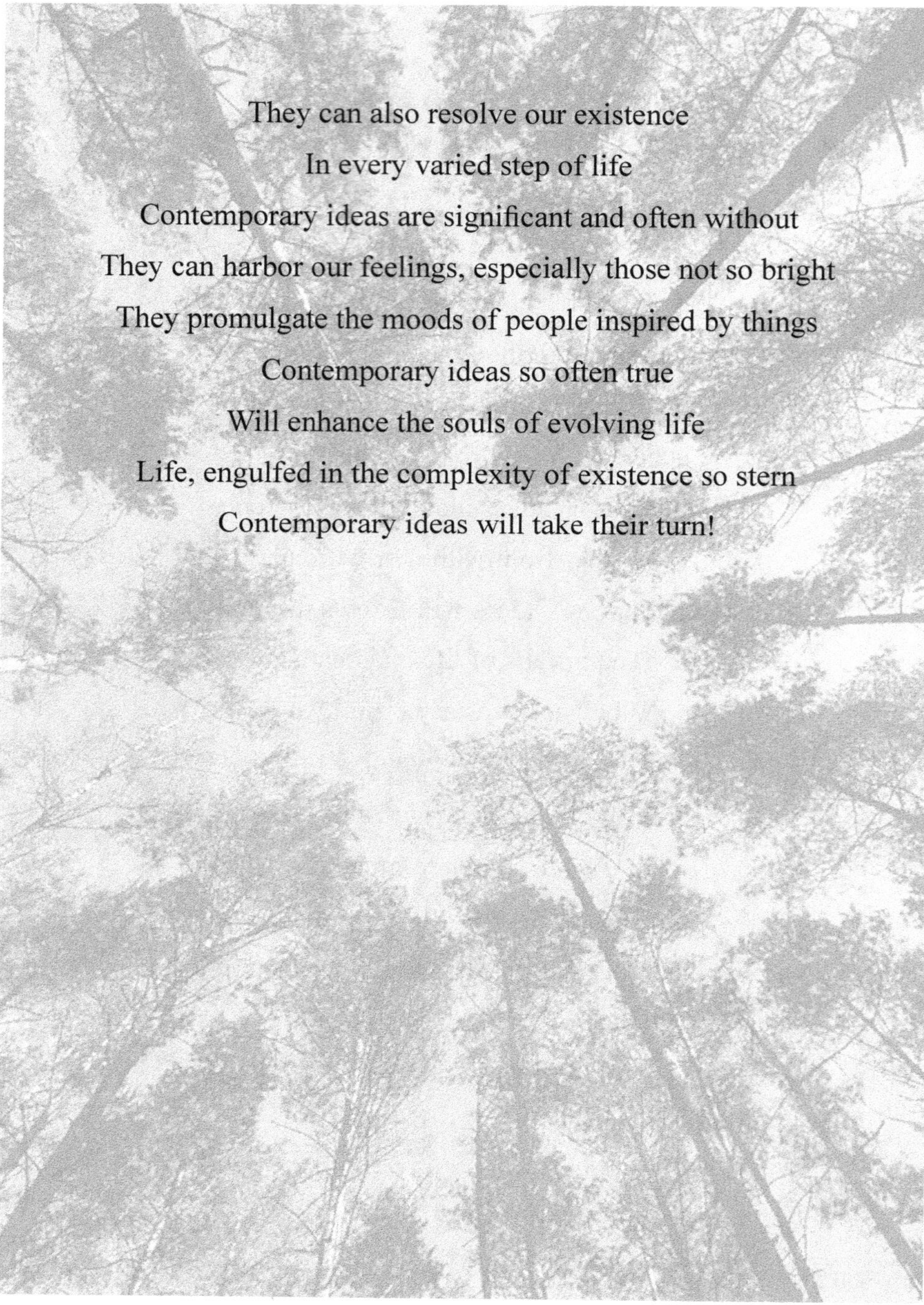

They can also resolve our existence

In every varied step of life

Contemporary ideas are significant and often without

They can harbor our feelings, especially those not so bright

They promulgate the moods of people inspired by things

Contemporary ideas so often true

Will enhance the souls of evolving life

Life, engulfed in the complexity of existence so stern

Contemporary ideas will take their turn!

DREAMING

A flight to Lisbon or
A ship to Marseilles
All within my reach
I dream about such things
Day after day, even at night
The desert, mine to touch
The mountains close by
Dreams intensify my life
Each brightens my day because
They are within my scope
And I dream so vividly
As each emits a ray of hope!

ECHOES

The echoes from afar and distant past
Cling to my lasting, intriguing thoughts
They remain within and always last
Embellishing my life like ocean troughs

Wherein those echoes erupt in dreams
To haunt my reverie, attained in sleep
They bind my life like flowing streams
To give my life rich rewards to reap!

ECESSIVE

Is life excessive?

No, I believe it is not

There is nature, there is work, and there is travel

People supplant the vacancies left by life's void

Nature's beauty, and its mountains or lakes

With their compensation, assuage the excesses

The frustration ordained by the strains of life,

The fruition rendered by positives

Have ruled with a beauty that compensates,

Then rules over the deviations engendered through haste

The excessive is our own frustration rendered and

Bred through an often-degenerating societal brood!

EXEMPLIFY

Exemplify that which is good
Show it through humility and finesse
Route the strength of the soul
Enhance the inner self
But remember, it is for one's own good
We cannot set aside the stress and challenges
Because they enhance the mystery of the soul
Show the creativity, enhanced by self-evaluation
Shoulder the burdens of rejection
Because through them, we can ascend again
Ascend again, to the glories of success,
And there the rewards of recognition can exemplify the soul!

FLIGHT ABROAD

The plane was crowded
But with all mostly teachers
Some female, some male
Over sixty of us, eager to explore
The engines, propeller driven,
Droned on and on!

The stops were to be short,
The salt winds of Bermuda
Awakened us for the evening pause
Only brief encounters with base personnel
Board again, with eyes on the Azores
Again, the engines droned on and on!

With an early breakfast stop,
After the night's long flight
Sleepy eyes seeing only the night
An endless night of clouds below
The island sighted, with lights very dim
But the engines still droned on!

With military personnel eager to greet us,
With kindness and to see new faces,
We departed the plane for the coffee and food
Hoping to hear tales of our destination to come
Even winds and rain soften the noise
Of the engine's constant drone that still went on!

On board again, with the sun clearing the sky
To carry the teachers to their destination
In a land so strange and large
With its location in the northern part
Of a continent that kissed the Mediterranean
But the engines' noise still droned on and on!

Many hours with youthful educators
Exchanging ideas brought from homes
In so many states,
Trying to adjust to the coming test of a new culture
Awaiting our intrusive views
But the engines' noise continued on!

Landing was soon and we knew that
The sands of the desert would kiss the sea

In a city called Tripoli
The country of Libya awaited our tales
To children of military stamped by America's brand
But the engines stilled droned on and on!

The final destination finally appeared
Through the plane's windows
Presenting sea and sand
With palm trees and camels for our view!
With Arabic tongues awaiting our teachers
But the engines diminishing drone still went on!

The quietness of the plane's extinguished noise
The doors opened widely to let us explore
A new land and culture to all of us new!
Now we could enter into jobs to teach abroad
With the hopes of experiences coming soon
With the noise of the plane no longer droning on and on!

FRIENDS

Friends in life expand our realm,

They enhance our existence

Even through trials of life

Proving our goals are worthy of strife-

Friends who are true are limited in numbers

But those who remain, are often few

So often the circle diminishes as we mature and grow!

Friends who remain during our path of life

Expand our universe, emitting a glow,

Imbued by richness, devoid of thorns!

Friends cast a glow on our paths, enlightening our being,

Because they emit a light that shows the way,

Through life's challenges or pleasures,

These few friends enrich our lives day by day!

GIGI

1/16/05

She appeared, sitting like an angel
An angel from a Latin land
And certainly, that she was, her hair so red
I thought, this must be a dream
A dream for sure and I danced with her
Just to be sure this wonder was true
What a rare moment it was for me
A lady from Ecuador far to the south
So statuesque and figure so divine
How can I capture this lady so great?
"Just ask her," said the guitarist
She is so Latin and refined I thought
"She will talk with you for sure," he said
"It is your chance of a lifetime"
And that was my queue!
I went to her, conversed and now
I know she is in my life awhile
And will always remain in my mind
Her vision will never die!

LIVING ABROAD

"Why, why? Why do you wish to live so far away"?
So many times the questions did come to me
They came to me in many forms;
"Are you not happy in your provincial setting"?
"Why do you desire living in another land"?

The questions came so often; sometimes veiled
And sometimes direct, but quite often open and true
"What draws you to other lands with languages anew"?
"Is it the challenge of people of different ways and
Roads that led to ancient civilizations?

The answers now remain within my mind
The travels and languages so new were embedded
And cast so tightly in memories of expanded past
They often flash by my brain; as though I never new
Those lands, people, and speech were in my mind to stay!

MOONLIGHT

It is often by moonlight
That I see the beauty of our world
When the night appears friendlier
Inspired by nature's way
Revealed by a light near my soul

Will moonlight inspire me
Throughout my life
And influence my thoughts
That I leave along the way
Or probe me like a dream

Moonlight, I spied
Only a few nights ago
Drifting above a great
And ancient oak and
Reigned like a golden charm

That moonlight emitted in gold
Showed life in its splendor
Evolving forever in my thoughts
To interweave my mode
On a glowing, eternal way!

MUSIC IN OUR LIVES

Why does music make our lives so bright?

If it is the band that plays or the orchestra that sounds

Either can shift our moods in many ways

If it is a voice behind or an instrument so acute

Either can enhance or dampen our moods

Through the years, composers have influenced

Not only our lives but nations near and afar

The sounds that come and go will stay

And keep us intact for eternal life,

To ease the pain and strife of another day!

MY PRINCESS

I cast my eyes on a soul so rich,

Imbued by God's perfect blend

As my care and love are rendered with

Complete devotion and care,

Never to be challenged by a questioning fear

From this one and only princess

Brought to me by a mystic so dear!

Now I place my heart within her realm,

My soul in complete admiration

Of her exotic charm

Because this princess is imbued

By a magic and unusual exotic blend

That only a few can comprehend!

MYSTERIES OF THE UNIVERSE

Mysteries of the universe permeate the night
The planets and stars continue to evolve
In a symbol of depth and complexity
The bodies that appear in the heavens
In a distance complex and far
With questions evoked by science!
The depth of the mystery will drive us
Someday, to distances not yet attained
But that void of perfection on earth,
The challenges of the mysterious universe
Will have to wait
Until the conflicts on earth
Evolve to a level yet not attained
But until mankind defines ita goals
And achieves them in full,
The mysteries of the universe
Will have to wait!

NEW ORLEANS, OUR CITY

The storm came in the night

Then hit with a mighty force

This region with its culture unique

But now nature has taken away

All the charm that kindled our souls

With a Cajun beauty that yearned to stay

Now a massive effort must make it right

This wonderful city, New Orleans

With its food and wine, must return again

To bestow to us, its lovely charms

Then our city will greet us with open arms!

NINA'S CHARM

On our first encounter, her eyes never met mine
She saw only the band, and heard sounds from the past
Her charm was obvious, with chemistry there,
A sincere and caring way with sincerity so rare,
My eyes saw only one, petite and well groomed
Then as I approached and asked for the dance,
She didn't say no, her quality emitted in her eyes,
A lady so true to her southern way,
She danced with a firm grasp of my hand,
With exuberance so fine and a swing of her arm,
As her rhythmic moves kept me aware
Of the vigorous flow of Nina's charm!

NOSTALGIA

Nostalgia resides within us all
Its peace and beauty console us nobly
Memories of places are now faded but refuse to leave
Faces evolve with age and renown
Erupting with tales so long gone
The chances of renewal and rebirth
Of days gone by, with events so long past
Will emerge with a force that seeks release
And often create the splendor within our hearts
The remnants of those before, some now gone,
Often connect and value the content
But some ignore the richness of the chance
To connect with nostalgia so rich and great
That renews the glow of a past so bright!

OTHER CULTURES

Other cultures seem to frustrate our security

Whether in travel or confrontations

One can alleviate the complexity rendered by the strange

And often seemingly different types about us

By approaching them through travel, study, or observation

Their existence need not be tread upon because of insecurity

Hasten to understand, hasten to explore, hasten to accept

For it is from us that the chain must be broken

If not, only utter chaos can challenge our progress

Through confrontation, acceptance, and trust,

Can we eliminate the true barriers of ones from afar?

Nature's perplexities render a veil of fear and distrust

Open the gate, though it is heavy, and once it is done,

The beauty and understanding will diminish the scorn of distrust!

OUR HEARTS ARE YOUNG

The years gone by are rich with love
The days of youth still linger in our hearts
The past is great with songs and memories
That invigorate our lives today, so that
We redeem a past so great and warm
Those times so rich and never escape
They make the essence of days gone by
Then enhance our being with endless life
The young view their future and we the past
But they too will someday look back and say
It was great and full of love forever to last!

OUR SPIRITS REVIVED

Dedicated to Irene

Our life each day is filled with love

Love from many friends along our way

Each life viewed from God above

Protecting us so we can never stray

From the friendships we cherish with care

Then hold them up with ties that bind

And renew those attachments once so rare

Our thoughts always of those who were so kind!

PERSUASION

When we use persuasion, to persuade or dissuade
It invades peoples' souls with strong intent
Persuasion erupts with firm and solid bent
It attacks many with convincing form
A tool utilized with technique and skill
Persuasion must be utilized with a tone
Of softness and everlasting concern
Or it will lack the finesse intended
For success and righteous appeal
Persuasion must not be delayed
Because it seeks the road of certain
Eventual needs for goals not yet seen!

PLEASURES

Pleasures are frequent in life
They exist in many forms,
Often found day by day
They lurk in every corner of life
Often too obscure for the hasty,
But distinct for those aware
Pleasures exist throughout our world,
Sometimes obviated by scorn, hate, or disdain
But pleasures return in full rapture,
Like a glowing poetic refrain!

REWARDS

My time is of the essence

My days are golden and unencumbered

The world has challenges yet to be met

Slumber, all of you who do not partake

The rewards awaiting will refresh my mind,

Because they are rich and kind

I shall not hesitate to fulfill my dreams

Because they fill the longing of my soul!

RUSH TO THE DAM

A rush to the dam,
For glory and fame in the fall
To catch the fish that really counts
The anglers turn out
With dreams so great
And optimism so bright!

A rush to the dam
The fish explore
The patience of the angler
Awaiting the lure
That will hook the trout
And secure its hold!

A rush to the dam
The prize of the day
That will hold its weight
In a drastic way
And make the count
That consumes the trait!

A rush to the dam

For residual trout,

And those who fish so diligently

From the fish planted in the spring

The fish remaining

Will enhance the string!

The dam is huge,

The water below

Will endure the persons

Fishing with vim and vigor

Within the flow

The fish are awaiting the eventual throw!

A place of refuge for those

Who fish with a source of know

And those who cast for the gradual glow

From the catch of the day

And eventual know

The dam above with its water below!

SEASONS

Seasons come in and out

Like journeys in our lives

They set our moods and calm our fears

Like ocean waves billowing toward the shore

Seasons console, inspire, and sometimes disrupt

The very inner selves of content souls

They sometimes set the mode

Of everyday tasks at hand

Sometimes evolving from gray to bright

Seasons often extend the limits

Of our psychic and extend

The boundaries of our flight!

SELF GUILT

My guilt was acquired in a world complex

Its halo surrounds me from its inception

Morality seeks its boundaries

From childhood, chastisement from within and without

The structure imbued with fundamental fervor

And devils devour the modes toward freedom

To survive the self-guilt chains enduring

And constrictions imposed in innocent molding,

One must view the world of natural morality,

Imposed through the flow of natural balance,

Then seek to release the chains so binding,

With a new inception, almost adolescent,

For lasting wisdom and eternal release,

From that world imposed by hypocritical indoctrination,

Until the chains of guilt are naturally eroded!

SHE AND I

1/19/05

She and I can be delightfully compared

She, so blonde and beautiful

I, grey and desirous, many years gone by

She dances with the spirit of an angel

I guide her moves with loving care

She, so erect, with grace given by

God I can only admire her endless charms

She, with an intellect of unending depth

I admire her with intuitive delight

She, alone, can satisfy my needs,

I pursue her love, seemingly eternal

She, full of charm and grace

Makes me dream she is in my life to stay

She alone fulfills my every longing

She and I, so much alike in every way!

SOUNDS IN THE NIGHT

The wind whistles through the trees,

Leaving the night with a sudden embedded refrain

The gentleness of nature's soft cry from

Many sorts of life, varied in air, earth and sky

Penetrating man's modest edifices, dwarfed by

Our globe's own monuments, girdled and eroded

From nature alone, but dominant until the end

Who knows what forms may be suddenly exposed

Through the whistles, cries, and pleas

All with reverence from within and without

But man alone cannot intrude into the

Illusions cast by the sounds in the night!

STARS, MARS, AND A FROSTY NIGHT

As I cast my eyes toward the distant sky
On a frosty September night,
I catch the twinkling of a myriad of stars
Among heaven's bright light
My eyes then drift to the brightest of all
For it imbues my soul within and without,
Far greater than the stars or a frosty night
The magnificent thing that glows above
Is our solar neighbor
Mars that appears so near
To our home on earth, above the stratosphere!

STRANGENESS OF THE HUNT

I am here in a land so different, but yet so similar

The guns of quality, the birds of the field

The beaters with a language in its Germanic vibration

The landowners with complete control

The shooters, all elite, of another vintage from which I come

The sound of the dogs, trained so well

Why do they not run away?

The complete control, the studied Jäger or hunter in my terms

Must rule the day

The organization, the control, so strange for us from another land

The chill of the November morn,

A Schnaps to warm the soul, a lingering talk with another hunter

Conservation, the methodology of the German mind

So detached from my hunting friends back home

But after years past and a reflection back, with progress

And crowded hunts to come,

The emergence of ecology so extreme!

SUMMER'S DYING GRASP

As summer fades away

The dying heat revels on,

Escape from its chains

Are enjoyed by a jubilant few

But we who remain with no say,

Must endure summer's grasp

In the realm of that captive vice,

Only to moan from its dismay

The elite who can choose their place,

Then boast and roar in their glee

Can evade nature's cruelty,

But those of us who must endure,

Seek escape from nature's grasp,

Through altered schemes to change

Natures hold with its unaltered rein!

THE ANGLER'S DREAM

The streams and lakes reflect the sky
Ripples spring forth as the trout arise
The dreams of anglers amplify the air
With spirits adrift amid the sky
A haven of peace set aside by forests green
Casting lines with lures aloft
Enhance the waters so pure
The trout's open eyes gaze
Quickly above the still pools, sparkling bight
The minnows, flies, and insects move in turmoil
As they escape the consuming fish
But nature's haven holds fast
The angler's dream of that waiting cast!

THE CHALLENGE OF OUR LAND

Our nation was born and set

In a land teemed with challenges

To be met by people from far away

Today it keeps its promises

Seeded by the rights of man,

Never lost or scarred

Through those who led,

But we must never forget,

The hunger of distrustful leaders

Who could lose our tradition

Through intangible amounts of greed!

THE EXOTIC LADY

1/15/05

The meeting was warm and cheerful
Her eyes green and appealing
The first encounter, cautious and tender
My feelings at first, only casual
Then within the conversation,
A significant turn of events
The mind of one who had seen
A world full of life, tested and tried
She captured my soul within a moment
Would she be the one?
Then later encounters, proved to be,
Not just a fleeting moment
But a promise for me!

THE HOUSE ON LOMBARDY LANE

It was my time of life, so vivid in my mind
A time of impressions so clear and deep
My time to move and find the home
The home and house to suit our style
My family only with impressions to gain
From the house that sat on Lombardy Lane!

The street so great in style and grace
Not a real street but one called a lane
The house with class and style kept my wants
Alive with anticipation; oh but to live there
Gave me the boost of desire and gain,
If only to live in the house on Lombardy Lane!

My friends were eager for that move
And family so true, brothers and sisters
Ready to venture in a residence so great
We were eager for the place of dreams

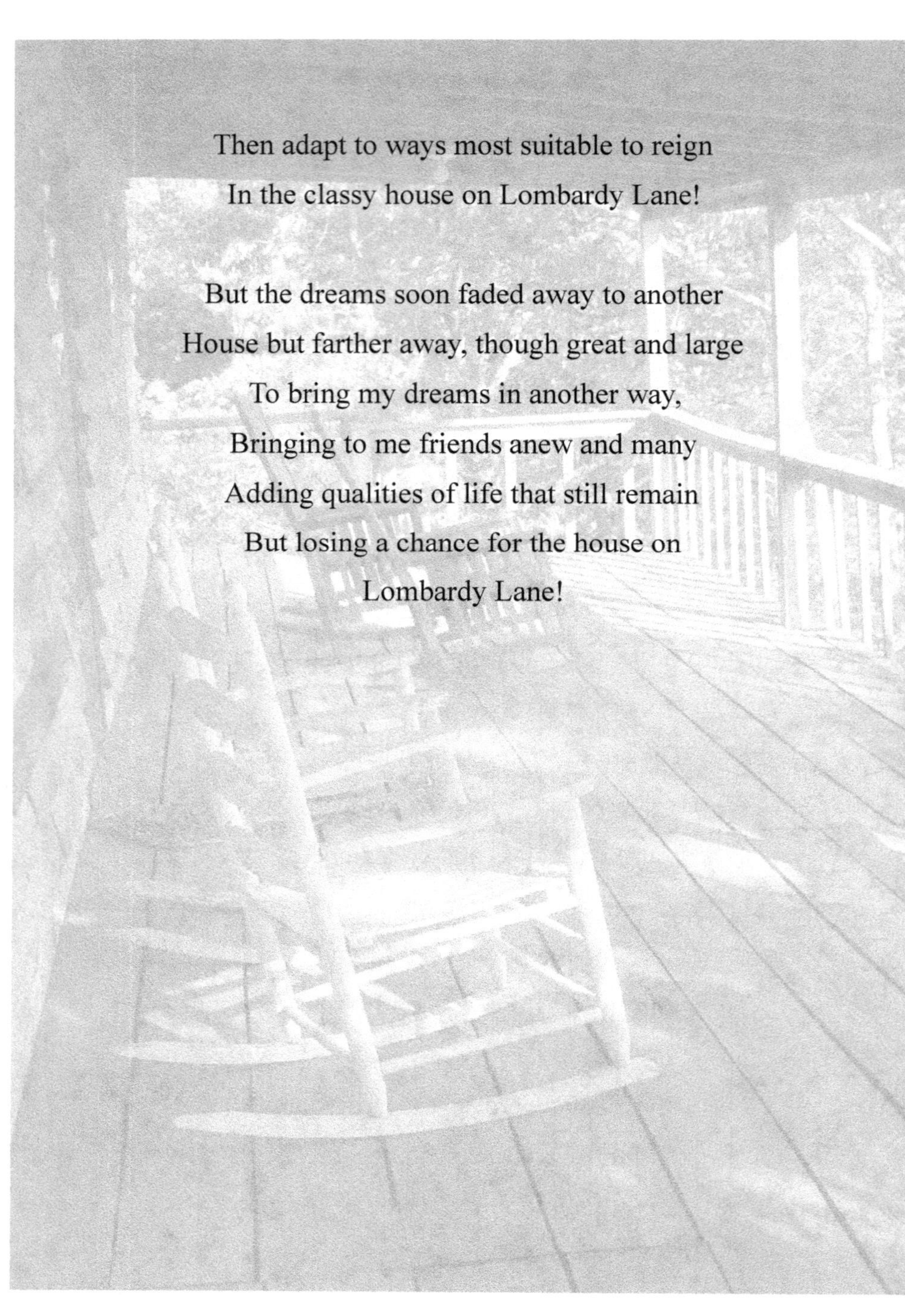

Then adapt to ways most suitable to reign
In the classy house on Lombardy Lane!

But the dreams soon faded away to another
House but farther away, though great and large
To bring my dreams in another way,
Bringing to me friends anew and many
Adding qualities of life that still remain
But losing a chance for the house on
Lombardy Lane!

THE MATRIARCH

Dedicated to Wanda Stell,

my sister, deceased February 3, 2003

A lady embarked on life's journey

With energy abound

She found her mate stern and bright

To guide and work with her in

The joyous streams of life

And together, wife and man closely bound

With a religious faith within their vows of love,

In full harmony, were imbued with a guided light!

She, with him, built a family of strength,

The matriarch of her family with stern demands,

But with love for her children and her mate

Never imparting scenes of hate,

Her love, through God, gave her strength

To endure and provide for a family innately sound,

So the father and children were fortified with love

Because of the matriarch's guidance from above!

TIMELINE

As I sit in solitude and reflect the past
The vision I see in days gone by
Moves from an era of things quite clear
To the dust of unpaved streets
With farmers who bartered for food,
Then the depression abruptly left
Because of bombs from the Orient so deft
And later the persecutions of dictators
From our European neighbors afar,
Each so stern, with control of all
The lands fell, swift and sudden
The Anglos abroad,
Brought justice to light
The end alerted the world at hand
That America was a righteous land
Today the timeline moves on
And for most, the just for a world for all!

TRANSCEND BEYOND

As night appears and dreams evolve

The mysteries on earth become intense

But light maintains its gracious glow

Only enough to rise, then gain resolve

Just as success in life is hard to achieve

And those who fail, cry out like a child

But the few who succeed will guide the way

Then rewards will emerge along the paths

The ones who escape the chains of life

Will fight their way and rightly respond

To open the way, then transcend beyond!

TRAVELS

A world so vast and beautiful
One wonders if all is to be seen
To ascend the mountains and plains
Takes more than just a simple try
But efforts great and desires beyond

To leave our setting, so peaceful and secure
Entails the dreams beyond the vast parade
Of security and a home of dreams
The mountains and plains, oceans too
Will be the challenge within our mark at last!

VARIABLES

Each one of us has his or her variables in life These variables are often subtle and intense.

These variables can complicate the day With each variable taking its toll Sometimes destructive or sometimes good Who knows the true effect?

The numerous changes that occur in life May present the moment of creative pomposity,

Poised and subtle, set to ignite

A soul of intensity, severed only by night!

VISIONS

Visions of nature so beautiful and pure
Her cloak of color and personality in the fall
The tint of the trees, the camouflage of her creatures
Trying to blend with the tones set by her stamp
Awaiting winter's cool hints of change
The mountains old and new, challenge man and game
The valleys invite them in a subdued manner
Her lakes blend with the earth colored with minerals so worn
The rain that cools the crust, filled with life of varying forms,

Visions of nature so colored by the storm
Her cloak of mist, sometimes ghostlike in its tone
The fields cast with green in the spring; robust in the fall,
Harboring various forms of life, plumed in dull and bright,
All in balance with earth's cover, food, and support
The trees that border fields, then tower so high,
The blend of the many aspects of nature do support
The visions perceived by man alone
Then hoist our life for sights to sort

WITHIN MY SCOPE

3.15.14

Within my scope of irrevocable dreams
Lies the wherewithal to explore beyond
Beyond that which is real, and about us now
Whether it be the universe at large or
Just the world within, one must know how far to go

Go beyond that, which is real or a dream beyond,
The soul of man will make its mark and limits to all
And carry out the expands of man beyond his soul
The caverns of the universe must open our minds
Then allow the scope of all to follow our dreams!

THE AUTHOR

Poetry has become a passion for me. I love to write about life, love, and the soul. After spending twenty-five years in Europe, I have returned to the United States and pursued writing poetry and books. Poetry is an avenue of release for me, giving me a chance to share my thoughts with others.

My childhood was spent in Arkansas (1932-1957) In Little Rock, completing high school, now Little Rock Central High. My parents owned grocery stores in Tinsman, Warren, and Little Rock and also owned a 1,000 acre tree farm near Tinsman, Arkansas.

I am a Korean Veteran and served with the U. S. Navy (1952-54), for which I am very proud; serving a short time on the USS Yorktown; air division as an Airman.

My teaching career spans Arkansas, New Orleans, Libya, North Africa, Germany, Italy, and The Netherlands. (1960-1986) I taught high school for 15 years, to 2001 in San Diego-Poway School District, then most of my time 1988-2001 teaching in secondary schools with San Diego Unified District.

In 1960 I received my master's degree from Vanderbilt University, Nashville, Tennessee, after which I was recruited while substitute teaching in Glendale, California to teach in secondary schools for in the above named countries, with the Department of Defense (Air Force and Army bases).

From 1977-1984 my wonderful task was teaching the Germans (evening school) in the German Volkshochschule for seven years, Bad Kreuznach, Germany, where I still have family ties; a daughter and former wife, both with successful businesses in Germany, along the Nahe River.

My greatest joys in life are returning to Bad Kreuznach, Germany and conversing in German with many of my old friends with whom I hunted, enjoyed white Riesling wines with, along the Nahe River. Karlsruhe, Germany was also a place I lived for five years hunting along the Rhine River.

www.ingramcontent.com/pod-product-compliance
Lightning Source LLC
Chambersburg PA
CBHW072051150726
47999CB00002B/993